It's an Event When We Experiment!

Kelly Doudna

Consulting Editors, Diane Craig, M.A./Reading Specialist
and Susan Kosel, M.A. Education

Published by ABDO Publishing Company, 4940 Viking Drive, Edina, Minnesota 55435.

Printed in the United States.

Credits
Edited by: Pam Price
Curriculum Coordinator: Nancy Tuminelly
Cover and Interior Design and Production: Mighty Media
Photo Credits: AbleStock, BananaStock Ltd., Corbis Images, ImageState, Photodisc, ShutterStock, Wewerka Photography

Library of Congress Cataloging-in-Publication Data

Doudna, Kelly, 1963-
    It's an event when we experiment! / Kelly Doudna.
     p. cm. -- (Science made simple)
    ISBN 10 1-59928-598-3 (hardcover)
    ISBN 10 1-59928-599-1 (paperback)

    ISBN 13 978-1-59928-598-6 (hardcover)
    ISBN 13 978-1-59928-599-3 (paperback)
    1. Science--Experiments--Juvenile literature. 2. Science--Juvenile literature. I. Title.

    Q182.3.D659 2007
    507.8--dc22

                                                                    2006021171

SandCastle Level: Transitional

SandCastle™ books are created by a professional team of educators, reading specialists, and content developers around five essential components—phonemic awareness, phonics, vocabulary, text comprehension, and fluency—to assist young readers as they develop reading skills and strategies and increase their general knowledge. All books are written, reviewed, and leveled for guided reading, early reading intervention, and Accelerated Reader® programs for use in shared, guided, and independent reading and writing activities to support a balanced approach to literacy instruction. The SandCastle™ series has four levels that correspond to early literacy development. The levels help teachers and parents select appropriate books for young readers.

Emerging Readers
(no flags)

Beginning Readers
(1 flag)

Transitional Readers
(2 flags)

Fluent Readers
(3 flags)

These levels are meant only as a guide. All levels are subject to change.

An **experiment** is the test of a hypothesis. The test is a series of steps that you do to find out information. At the end of the experiment, you report the results.

These words are used to talk about an experiment:

conclude **results**
hypothesis **test**
learn **variable**

I do an experiment to learn if need sunlight to grow.

I put one plant by the and the other in the closet.

I do an experiment to learn how far my toy will roll.

First I roll the

on the dining room

 . Then I roll it on

the kitchen floor.

I do an experiment

to learn what kind

of food my

likes best.

The of dry food is still full. I conclude that my likes canned food because that is empty.

It's an Event When We Experiment!

Walter and Wanda
want to know
how small the
shadow will go.
They've made a guess,
and now they'll
do the test.

When the light moves away, we think that the size of the shadow will shrink.

They use flashlights and balls to cast shadows on the wall. They keep the balls in the same place while they move one light in space.

The only variable we alter is where the lights are held by Walter.

First Walter takes aim,
and then Wanda
does the same.
They repeat the action
to see if they get the
same reaction.

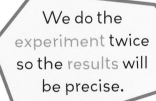

We do the experiment twice so the results will be precise.

We Experiment Every Day!

Wei wants to know if the size of a balloon affects how far it will float.

Wei experiments by letting balloons of two different sizes go in the wind.

Tim's hypothesis is that a big stone will make a bigger splash than a small stone.

Tim and his dad do an experiment. First Tim throws a small stone. Then his dad throws a large stone.

These friends want to know whether the basketball or the soccer ball will bounce higher.

They experiment by dropping each ball from the same height.

Jackie wonders how long water takes to cool in the refrigerator.

How could Jackie experiment to learn the answer?

Glossary

alter – to change.

conclude – to make a judgment after reasoning and thinking carefully.

hypothesis – a statement that seems to explain a set of facts and is the basis for an experiment.

result – something that happens because of what someone or something does.

shrink – to become smaller.

variable – something that changes.